HAYN **W9-BBP-999** RE

Systems of Government

MONARCHY

Sean Connolly

Smart Apple Media

Published by Smart Apple Media, an imprint of Black Rabbit Books
P. O. Box 3263, Mankato, Minnesota 56002
www.blackrabbitbooks.com

Library of Congress Cataloging-in-Publication Data
Connolly, Sean, 1956-
 Monarchy / by Sean Connolly.
     p. cm.—(Systems of government)
 Includes index.
 Summary: "Describes the government workings of a monarchy, including the
differences between a constitutional monarchy and the more rare absolute monarchy.
The history of how monarchies have evolved, the role of monarchs today, and the
future of monarchies are examined"—Provided by publisher.
 ISBN 978-1-59920-805-3 (library binding)
 1. Monarchy—Juvenile literature. I. Title.
 JC375.C656 2013
 321.8'7--dc23
                        2011040092

Created by Appleseed Editions, Ltd.

Designed by Hel James
Edited by Mary-Jane Wilkins
Picture research by Su Alexander

Picture credits
page 5 Getty Images; 7 Thinkstock; 9 Photos.com/Thinkstock; 10 MCT via
Getty Images; 12 Getty Images; 14 Dutourdumonde/Shutterstock; 16 Tim Graham/
Getty Images; 18 Getty Images; 20 Tim Graham/Getty Images; 23 Getty Images;
25 Photos.com/Thinkstock; 26 Tim Graham/Getty Images; 30 WireImage/Getty
Images; 31 AFP/Getty Images; 32 Tim Graham/Getty Images; 34 & 36 AFP/Getty
Images; 38 & 40 Getty Images; 43 AFP/Getty Images; 45 Tim Graham/Getty Images

Printed in the United States of America at Corporate Graphics,
North Mankato, Minnesota
PO1445
2-2012

987654321

Contents

Monarchy and Tradition

In a world of iPads and virtual reality, sometimes it seems hard to believe that kings and queens still exist except as part of a computer game or a costume party. However, nearly 50 countries still have a monarchy with a king or queen at the heart of its government.

It is even more surprising that many people living in those countries believe their system to be fair and just. The Dutch, for example, believe that their nation is one of the most forward-looking and tolerant societies in the world. Yet they live in a monarchy. Canadians live in a wide-open country that has the skyscrapers, big cars, and glamour of its US neighbor. Yet the Canadian **head of state** is the monarch on the throne more than 3,100 miles (5,000 km) away in Britain.

Those countries, like most of the world's monarchies, have succeeded in introducing the best aspects of representative governments (such as fair elections and a **free press**) while preserving the sense of history and tradition that reassures many people living in monarchies. Even the monarchies that have done less to move into the modern era can claim to provide the right government for their people, based on the same reasons of history and tradition.

Shared Background

Like many words used to define other types of government, the word monarchy comes from the Greek language. It is derived from the Greek words *monos arkhein*, meaning one ruler. Most monarchies were established after a single ruler emerged from power struggles to rule over a nation.

Many monarchies have similar origins even if the original power struggles were centuries ago. Today, though, there is no single

TIMELINE... TIMELINE... TIMELINE... TIMELINE... TIMELINE... TIMELIN'

3500 BC   Egypt united under King Menes   2551   Khufu becomes **pharaoh**; builds Great Pyramid

blueprint for monarchies in the modern world. Each one has chosen—or been forced—to change in some way. In some modern societies, the monarch is elected. In others, the monarch stands apart from day-to-day politics as a sort of referee and national symbol. Each variation, however, tries to retain the sense of tradition that many find so important in a monarchy. This book examines how monarchies coexist with a fast-changing world. Could one of the oldest forms of government—which draws its strength from looking back—be the best one to look ahead into an unknown future?

The wedding of Prince William and Catherine Middleton in April 2011 captured the imagination of the British public. For many, this fairy tale wedding offered escape from the economic bad news.

TIMELINE... TIMELINE... TIMELINE... TIMELINE... TIMELINE... TIMELINE...

2070 Xia **Dynasty** begins in China, beginning a long line of Chinese dynasties

Tapping Tradition

An exchange between political leaders and the people of a country is at the heart of any type of government. A **democracy** is a great example. The people choose their leaders by elections. In return for being elected, the political leaders agree to guide the country sensibly. The alternative is clear: if they don't live up to expectations, they can be voted out of office.

It is harder to see the exchange in a monarchy, especially as the first monarchies rewarded the most powerful warriors with political power. Over the years, though, the number of **absolute monarchies** (see page 11) has diminished; kings and queens, emperors, and **emirs** have had to acknowledge the rights and wishes of their people. That acknowledgement forms part of the exchange that exists at the heart of monarchies today.

National Heritage

Most people like to feel proud of their country whether it is due to its sporting success, military victories, cultural history, or the character of its people. The desire to feel these strengths, which help define the country, runs deep. For example, for centuries French people have celebrated their skills in cooking, fashion, and a coolness under pressure. Greeks are proud of their contribution to thinking, architecture, and the arts. All these qualities make up a country's heritage.

Monarchies and the age-old systems they represent are an important feature in the heritage of many countries. Britain is one example. Tourists come from all over the world to see Buckingham Palace, the Changing of the Guard, and the treasures of the Tower of London. All are essential elements of the British monarchy. British people pay a great deal for this heritage, but that is where the exchange comes in.

In effect, British taxpayers provide the royal family with luxury, honor, and some responsibilities. In exchange, the royal family provides taxpayers with a link to the past and a powerful sense of the nation's heritage. The (usually) unspoken addition to such sentiment might be: "We also acknowledge that the pageantry and ceremonies attached to all this tradition have a healthy effect on our economy, and we feel that you contibute by attracting foreign visitors to our country."

This view of monarchy is the most common in the twenty-first century. It would be foolish of a newly independent country to create a monarchy and expect people to obey or even respect it. The attraction of a monarchy is its links with the past. Most people who live in this

Centuries-old ceremonies, such as Trooping the Colour (above), underpin the monarchy's role in British society.

TIMELINE... TIMELINE... TIMELINE... TIMELINE... TIMELINE... TIMELINE...

1047　Saul becomes first King of Israel　　930　Kingdom of Israel splits; both are conquered by 586

type of system today accept this state of affairs by either paying little attention to the monarchy (because real power is held by elected leaders) or by approving of people who act as national symbols.

Blurred Boundaries

Most countries with monarchies must address the fundamental question: Where does symbolism end and real power begin? Does the political system make it clear where those boundaries are? What would happen if a king or queen (or their representative) decided to enter the political battlefield? Many Australians believe that occurred in their country in 1975 (see page 28).

Less dramatically, Prince Charles has been accused of meddling when he has expressed strong views on architecture by possibly influencing government decisions on which architects to employ and how British cities should look. Then again, it can be argued that monarchies

HEAD OF STATE

Nearly every government of any type has a person who represents the state (nation) in public affairs. The famous French leader Charles de Gaulle described that role as embodying "the spirit of the nation." France no longer has a monarchy, but the French elect a president to act as their head of state. That role in Britain and in other monarchies is held by the reigning monarch.

Defenders of monarchy point out that a royal head of state (as opposed to an elected one) is not linked to divisive politics. In their view, Queen Elizabeth is an effective head of state because she stands outside politics. Unlike elected political leaders, she did not make promises (or enemies) to achieve her position. She inherited the position.

Opponents argue that being born to a job is no guarantee that someone can do that job well. Some might argue that although Elizabeth does a good job as queen, there is no guarantee that her son—or grandson—will do as good a job.

TIMELINE... TIMELINE... TIMELINE... TIMELINE... TIMELINE... TIMELINE

753 BC   Romulus (according to legend) becomes the first Roman king

have never been completely removed from the people. Britain's King George VI and his queen were welcome symbols of British spirit during London's darkest hours during **World War II**, so why should their grandson (Charles) stay out of the public eye? Britain's monarchy is not the only one that needs to balance progress and tradition. Every king, queen, prince, emir, **sultan**—even the pope—must be able to change with the times while symbolizing the past as well.

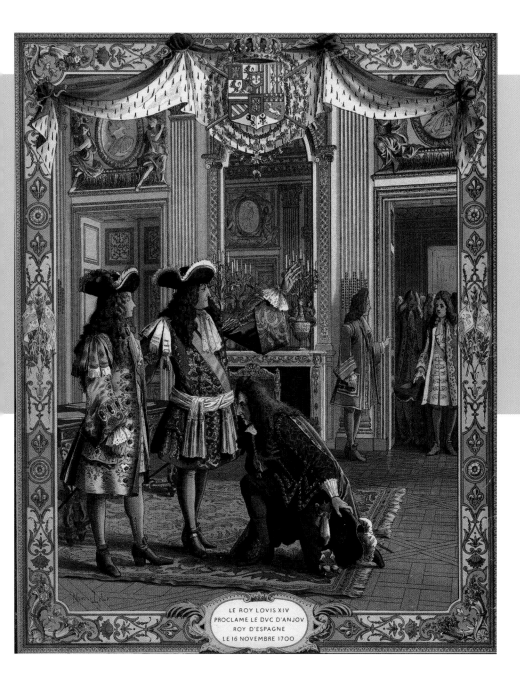

LE ROY LOVIS XIV
PROCLAME LE DVC D'ANJOV
ROY D'ESPAGNE
LE 16 NOVEMBRE 1700

Louis XIV reigned over France for 72 years in the seventeenth and eighteenth centuries. By forcing noblemen to live in his lavish palace of Versailles, Louis cleverly managed to keep an eye on potential threats to his power.

MELINE... TIMELINE... TIMELINE... TIMELINE... TIMELINE... TIMELINE...

660 Japanese monarchy founded and is the world's oldest existing monarchy

Might versus Right

One drawback of any elected government is
that it can take a long time to make or change laws.
When US President Barack Obama was elected in 2008,
he promised to reform the country's medical system so
that more Americans would receive medical insurance.
As his opponents fought every attempt to make those
changes, the idea was debated repeatedly in the
US **Congress**.

TIMELINE... TIMELINE... TIMELINE... TIMELINE... TIMELINE... TIMELIN

509 BC   Roman monarchy abolished   332   As part of his conquest of the Persian Empire, Alexander the Great

Eventually the **bill** was passed, but it took nearly 15 months to reach that point. By the time it passed, Obama and his supporters in Congress had to agree to a number of **compromises** that severely limited the original idea. Few were really happy with this. Strong supporters of reform regretted the way in which Obama had been forced to give ground on so many issues. Opponents of reform wondered why Congress had spent so much time on the issue when it had more important matters to debate, including the economy.

Opponents of President Obama's health care proposals protest angrily in Washington. Supporters of monarchies argue that a king or queen can help soothe such national divisions and help people to find common ground.

What I Say Goes

Imagine what it would be like if leaders could say, "Those who disagree with me will be fined or jailed." An absolute monarch has that type of power. Most European monarchies began with rulers claiming absolute power. However, throughout the Middle Ages, influential **nobles** worked together to depose a king if they disagreed with his leadership.

European monarchs gained more power during the seventeenth and eighteenth centuries. This was due in large part as nations became more centralized and were more easily controlled by one person. Monarchs also gained power by raising taxes with less interference from the nobles. King Louis XIV of France summed up his position with two memorable phrases: *une foi, une loi, un roi* (one faith, one law, one king) and *l'etat, c'est moi* (the state, it is I). In this view of absolute monarchy, the king (or queen) is the element that holds the country together.

By the mid-eighteenth century, democratic ideas spread across Europe; most monarchies had to give away powers or face outright **revolution**. The seeds of the modern British system of **constitutional monarchy** (see pages 16–17) were sown at this time, and the reigning monarch assumed more of a symbolic role. Other monarchies held on to absolute power into the twentieth century. The Russian **tsar** continued to make many important government decisions up to the time of the Russian Revolution in 1917. Theoretically, the Japanese emperor (see page 13) was in charge of the branches of government—and even the state religion—until 1947.

Modern Examples

Today, only six countries—mostly small ones—can claim to be absolute monarchies, which means the monarch is head of both state and government. These countries are Brunei, Oman, Qatar, Saudi Arabia, Swaziland, and Vatican City. Pro-democracy elements have called for change—and have occasionally faced violent reaction from the police—in four of those countries. The exceptions are Vatican City, where most of the population is involved with the headquarters of the Catholic Church, and Brunei, whose small population is relatively well off because of the country's oil wealth.

Japan's Emperor Hirohito inspects bomb damage in Tokyo caused by an American bombing raid in October 1943.

305 BC   Ptolemy I Soter becomes pharaoh, starting the last age of Egyptian kings

"After Pondering Deeply. . ."

The term for the Japanese monarch is emperor although Japan did not have an empire for much of its history. The island nation began to expand greatly when it invaded China and much of southeast Asia in the 1930s, helping to trigger World War II. Japanese soldiers and ordinary people were prepared to die for their emperor, who was considered almost a god.

After the Americans dropped two massively destructive atomic bombs on Japanese cities in August 1945, it became clear that Japan would be defeated no matter what it did. Surrender was the only alternative, but that went against the Japanese code of honor.

Emperor Hirohito made the decision to surrender and announced to the Japanese people on the radio on August 15, 1945, "To our good and loyal subjects: after pondering deeply the general trends of the world and the actual conditions obtaining to our empire today, we have decided to effect a settlement of the present situation by resorting to an extraordinary measure. We have ordered our government to communicate to the governments of the United States, Great Britain, China, and the Soviet Union that our empire accepts the provisions of their joint declaration." (The provisions called for Japan's surrender.)

He chose not to use the word *surrender* in that opening and went on to say that Japan had only entered the war to protect itself. He noted the enemy used a cruel new weapon and said: "Should we continue to fight, it would not only result in an ultimate collapse and [destruction] of the Japanese nation, but also it would lead to the total extinction of human civilization."

The emperor had cleverly protected Japan's cherished sense of honor. According to him, Japan had entered the war in self-defense and had willingly ended it to protect human civilization. It is hard to imagine an elected leader getting away with those words and being believed by his people.

MELINE... TIMELINE... TIMELINE... TIMELINE... TIMELINE... TIMELINE...

AD 220   San Guo (Three Kingdoms) in China   581   Sui Dynasty begins in China

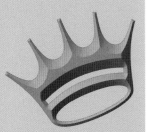

For king and country

We can learn a lot about how countries see themselves by listening to their national anthems. Many nations sing proudly of how they rid themselves of monarchies at some point in their history and how the governments which replaced those monarchies—according to the anthems—promote freedom and reflect the wishes of the people.

Argentina, ruled by the Spanish monarchy for centuries, celebrates its independence with the words:
"Mortals! Hear the sacred cry:
Freedom! Freedom! Freedom!"

France's violent revolution overthrew its monarchy. According to its national anthem, conservative European countries (including Great Britain) feared the demise of other monarchies and tried to quell France's new freedom:
"Arise children of the fatherland
The day of glory has arrived
Against us tyranny's
Bloody **standard** is raised."

The German anthem is less extreme but still celebrates "Unity and justice and freedom for the German fatherland." Compare those sentiments with the words of the British national anthem:
"Send her victorious,
Happy and glorious,
Long to reign over us:
God save the Queen."

Or the Japanese anthem:
"May thy peaceful reign last long!
May it last for thousands of years."

Neither the British nor the Japanese anthem mentions justice, freedom, equality, or liberty. Instead, they sing the praises of loyalty and tradition. The basis of the loyalty and tradition is the monarchy in each case. But do the British and Japanese consider themselves less free or more oppressed than the Argentineans, French, and Germans?

Subjects or Citizens?

Another way of looking at this issue is to see that the two systems aim for the same target—a just and fair society—but take different routes. A republic is typified by the French and American systems. Both countries rejected monarchy in the eighteenth century and produced documents stating how their governments would operate.

Even countries that have abolished their monarchies need symbols. The French use an idealized image of French womanhood, nicknamed Marianne, as a symbol of their nation. Instead of a crown, she wears the floppy cap that was popular during the French Revolution in the late eighteenth century.

Lords gather at the State Opening of Britain's Parliament. Can unelected noblemen have a role in a modern democracy?

The US Constitution, which was ratified in 1789, is still the supreme law of the United States. In 1789, about a month after the French Revolution had begun, France adopted the Declaration of the Rights of Man and of the Citizen. Like the American document, it announced that all people had basic rights and that governments could be chosen by those people to protect their rights.

Both these countries, and many others that followed their example, believed that a nation's people were equal in the eyes of the law. No one was superior or guaranteed special powers. The term *citizen* emphasized that. Although the French briefly brought back the monarchy in the nineteenth century, the idea of citizenship still remains at the heart of the French political system.

At that time, the British people were proud to consider themselves subjects rather than citizens. They heard of the violence surrounding the French Revolution—up to 40,000 French citizens were executed by the guillotine—and drew comfort from their secure monarchy.

Constitutional Monarchy

The British political system, unlike those in the United States and France, has no written constitution. Instead, the laws passed by Parliament and the decisions taken by British judges form what is often called an unwritten constitution. The British monarchy has evolved within such a system as parliamentary bills or legal judgements edge it in new directions.

The result is that the United Kingdom has a system called a constitutional monarchy, which is often seen as the opposite of an absolute monarchy. Most monarchies today are constitutional. The unelected head of state retains symbolic power; in reality, it is governed by the wishes of the elected political leaders. Supporters of such systems argue that this offers the best of all worlds. The voters choose leaders who have real power while the monarchy provides the tradition and heritage that many democracies lack.

THE VOTING BOOTH

Coexistence

Few people would argue that the reigning British monarch has real political power in the twenty-first century. But many opponents of the system argue that having an unelected head of state affects the way people view the entire system. For example, in their view, it justifies having an unelected section of the real political system (the House of Lords).

Can monarchy and democracy coexist? Will there always be a clash if some people are born into positions of power or honor?

...TIMELINE... TIMELINE... TIMELINE... TIMELINE... TIMELINE... TIMELINE...

924   Athelstan becomes king of England—accepted by many historians as the first king of England

Mixing It Up

There are no blueprints for the way monarchies operate. Some follow the British pattern of constitutional monarchy with a largely symbolic monarch acting as head of state and succeeding (taking over from) the previous monarch through **heredity**. Others elect their monarch or use different methods of royal succession. Some newly independent countries choose to maintain historical ties with other monarchies through associations such as the **Commonwealth of Nations**.

The Commonwealth

Driving across the border from the United States to Canada, visitors might find it difficult to spot any differences between the two countries. The cars look the same, the people sound the same, and there is a similar mix of forest and farmland as well as suburb and high-rise city skylines. But once US visitors stop to buy something, they will notice something very different.

Most Canadian coins are the same size and are of similar value to their American counterparts, but one side of Canadian coins depicts Queen Elizabeth II of Great Britain. However, the British no longer rule Canada as they once did. Canada is an independent country and makes its own

A spectacular closing ceremony brought an end to the 2010 Commonwealth Games in India. The games are similar to the Olympic Games and bring together teams from the 54 member nations of the Commonwealth.

ROYAL SUCCESSION

Queen Elizabeth II inherited the British throne when her father, King George VI, died in 1952. The British succession is based on heredity, which means that the heir to the throne becomes king or queen as soon as the reigning monarch dies. The phrase "The king is dead; long live the king!" sums up the advantage of a hereditary monarchy. The title passes smoothly and without disagreement from one person to another.

Heredity is not the only type of royal succession. Many monarchies have used elections to determine a new ruler. Assemblies in ancient Rome chose each new king (before Rome became a republic in 509 BC). A group of nobles, called prince-electors, chose the **Holy Roman Emperor** throughout much of the Middle Ages.

There are a few modern elected monarchies. Hereditary rulers of the nine Malay states elect a supreme head of state for a five-year term. The Royal Council of the Throne (made up of nobles with royal blood) chooses Cambodia's king for a life term. The **College of Cardinals** elects a successor when a pope dies.

decisions on national and international matters. It does, however, retain an important connection with Great Britain, which explains the image of the British monarch on its money.

The Commonwealth of Nations (Commonwealth for short) is a voluntary group of 54 independent nations that share values of freedom, justice, and cooperation. Most of the countries have historical ties with Great Britain, and, in many cases, were British colonies at one time. Canada is part of a smaller group of 16 nations called Commonwealth realms (countries that recognize the reigning British monarch as their head of state). This means that among her many titles, Elizabeth II is Queen of Canada.

Most Commonwealth realms also have elected governments similar to the British. Bills in Commonwealth realms need royal approval in the same way as bills passed in the British Parliament before they become law (see page 24). The monarch's representative, or **governor-general**, does the approving.

(see page 24)

TIMELINE... TIMELINE... TIMELINE... TIMELINE... TIMELINE... TIMELIN

AD 1271   Yuan Dynasty (founded by Mongol leader Kublai Khan) begins in China

OPPOSING THE MONARCHY IN AUSTRALIA

The Commonwealth realm with the most vocal anti-monarchy movement is Australia. Many Australians trace their ancestry to Ireland and resent the role Britain has played over the years. Australia has a strong trade union movement, which tends to oppose the "stuffiness" of royalty in general. More recently, Australians have begun to think of themselves as part of Asia's sphere rather than linked to the more distant Britain.

Most Australians who oppose the monarchy are republicans. They want Australia to be a **republic** (like France or the United States) with an elected head of state. Australia held a **referendum** in 1999 to find out whether voters wanted the country to become a republic. The proposal to change the existing system failed with 55 percent of the voters choosing the monarchy. Since then, the republican movement has gained some support. An August 2010 poll found that 48 percent of Australians wanted to keep the monarchy while 44 percent preferred a republican system.

Anti-monarchy protesters use their national holiday, Australia Day, to call for a republic to replace Australia's ties with the British monarchy.

VOICE OF THE PEOPLE

RESPECT FOR BETTY WINDSOR

When Queensland resident James MacPherson added his comments to a blog about Australia's monarchy, he came down on the side of a republic. However, he mixes this preference with some earthy admiration for the present British (and Australian) monarch, Queen Elizabeth II: "I hope that Australia becomes a republic, with a head of state elected by the people. I have the greatest respect for Betty Windsor [Queen Elizabeth, whose surname is technically Windsor] and the job that she has done as our monarch—Queen of Australia—but I despise and detest the concept of hereditary privilege, and I loathe the royal family."

TIMELINE... TIMELINE... TIMELINE... TIMELINE... TIMELINE... TIMELINE...

| 1297 | Grimaldi Dynasty begins in Monaco | 1350 | Siamese (Thai) kingdoms united under one throne |

Making a Monarchy Work

Very few monarchies have come into being since the seventeenth century. Some new monarchies have been formed partly by outside forces or as a result of wider political needs. Belgium became independent in 1830 at a time when major European powers tried to prevent any one country from becoming too powerful (as France had become under **Napoleon**). Yugoslavia was formed in 1918 by merging a number of states that had been part of the **Austro-Hungarian Empire**, which was broken up at the end of **World War I**.

Both Belgium and Yugoslavia chose to follow the example of Great Britain by becoming constitutional monarchies. The choice made sense. Supporters of monarchies argue that the head of state (the monarch) stands above the differences of political parties or nationalities that make up the nation. Queen Elizabeth II, for example, is not just monarch of the English, but of the Welsh, Scots, and some Irish (not to mention Australians, Canadians, New Zealanders, and others living in the Commonwealth realms).

Delicate Balance

Other monarchies have taken a thousand years or more to adopt the system that Belgium and Yugoslavia chose. These monarchies could not claim centuries of tradition, but their founders saw the value of having a monarch as a symbol of political neutrality at the head of a government.

In Britain, the queen supports the party that is in control. Every year, she outlines forthcoming political plans in the **Queen's Speech.**

TIMELINE... TIMELINE... TIMELINE... TIMELINE... TIMELINE... TIMELIN

AD **1368** Ming Dynasty begins in China **1375** Acamapichtli becomes first Aztec ruler

The fact that her speech is written by members of the ruling government (whichever political party has a **majority** in Parliament) shows exactly who makes the decisions that affect Britain. However, all the work of those elected officials—in Parliament and in government generally—is technically unofficial until the monarch agrees to it.

The accompanying chart shows how government plans (called bills) pass through Parliament before eventually becoming law. This process depicts the workings of a constitutional monarchy. With very few exceptions, every modern monarch deals with a similar combination of hands-off (in creating laws) and hands-on (in approving laws).

Indonesian President Susilo Bambang Yudhoyono addresses senators and members of the Australian Parliament in March 2010 during an official visit. Australian anti-monarchists feel that an Australian republic would be better placed to trade with its Asian neighbors.

1397   Danish and Norwegian monarchies unite   1469   Spanish kingdoms united under one throne

A BILL BECOMES LAW IN BRITAIN

House of Commons

First reading: A bill is introduced and will be discussed at an agreed second date.

Second reading: A minister introduces the bill. It is debated and voted on to determine if it will move on to further stages.

Committee stage: A small cross-party committee (15–50 members) is formed to discuss the bill in detail.

Report stage: The bill is reprinted, taking into account any suggested changes (amendments).

Third reading: This is the last chance for the Commons to vote on whether the bill should proceed further. If they vote yes, the bill goes to the House of Lords.

House of Lords

First reading: The bill approved by the Commons is introduced to be discussed at an agreed second date.

Second reading: The bill is discussed, but the Lords have far less scope for amendments than the Commons.

Report stage: Only if considered necessary.

Third reading: The final discussion and vote. If the majority vote yes, the bill only awaits the final stage.

Royal Assent

The monarch once signed each bill personally. Now the queen (or king) appoints special lords as Royal Commissioners to announce that Royal Assent has been granted. Only then does the bill become law.

Commonwealth countries have similar systems within their parliaments. In these countries, the governor-general (representing the British monarchy) provides the Royal Assent.

A Clash of Interests

The words of the French national anthem make it clear
that kings and queens are tyrants and cannot be trusted.
Their supporters are no better:
"Tremble, tyrants and traitors
The shame of all good men
Tremble! Your **parricidal** schemes
Will receive their just reward."

No doubt, those heated words suited the turbulent period of the French
Revolution and echoed across much of Europe and beyond. Many
believed that the rulers who inherited their position (rather than being
elected to it) would behave selfishly and cruelly. The only solution—and
the one chosen by the revolutionary French government—was to execute
monarchs and get rid of the old system.

*King Louis XVI is
executed at the guillotine
in Paris on January 21,
1793. From that point
on, there was no turning
back for the French
revolutionaries.*

Prince Charles visits Poundbury. The new town was built in his preferred architectural style and on his own land.

Beheading was one way of resolving clashes between monarchs and their subjects, but it is hardly a fitting solution in the twenty-first century. How do today's monarchies deal with disagreements between a monarch and his or her country?

Checks and Balances

The short answer is that monarchs know better than to upset the people. In most constitutional monarchies, the heads of state receive much of their income from those very people in grants and allowances that are determined by elected politicians. The heads of state are probably wealthy landowners in their own right (Prince Charles, for example, earns millions of pounds every year from his estates in Cornwall), but depend on taxpayers for much of their income.

TIMELINE... TIMELINE... TIMELINE... TIMELINE... TIMELINE... TIMELIN

AD **1603**   **English and Scottish kingdoms united under one throne**

MONSTROUS CARBUNCLE

Queen Elizabeth II is noted for her calm, correct behavior. She rarely shows emotion and has never been linked to a scandal that might trigger controversy. Her eldest son (and heir), Prince Charles, has been more forthright in expressing his opinions and has been criticized as a result.

The prince has generated debate after publicly stating his opinions on medicine, farming, and the teaching of English in schools. Perhaps his most famous public statements concern architecture. In 1984, he criticized plans to build a modern extension to the National Gallery, calling the proposed extension "a monstrous **carbuncle** on the face of a much-loved and elegant friend."

The comment sparked a fierce debate about the merits of modern versus old-fashioned architecture, but it went further than that. The prince's influence meant that other modern plans were quietly abandoned and the careers of many architects suffered as a result. Some architects remain bitter about Prince Charles's comments decades later.

Leading architecture critic Rowan Moore, writing in the London *Evening Standard* in 2009, summed up the bitterness: "The unelected prince, with a limited knowledge of architecture and planning and no accountability, became an unofficial additional organ of the planning system."

As well as the queen's personal income from property and investments (not funded by the public), she receives money from publicly funded sources such as:
- grant-in-aid for the upkeep of royal palaces;
- the Privy Purse for official spending; and
- the **Civil List** (which also funds other members of the **royal household**).

| 1613 | Mikhail Romanov becomes tsar of Russia | 1649 | King Charles I executed, ending English monarchy |

Each of these categories has been criticized at one time or another because of the amounts of money involved or because of negative reactions to the behavior of the royal family. Scandals involving present or former members of the royal family can trigger a public outcry about spending millions each year on them. As a rule, the Civil List triggers the most public disapproval, especially when economic times are difficult for most people. The result of this complicated system of payments and allowances is that the royal family must not provoke disapproval.

A Commonwealth Crisis

In late 1975, Australia's leading politicians were bitterly opposed on a number of issues, which included national borrowing, the appointment of ambassadors, and the calling of elections. Prime Minister Gough Whitlam of the Labor Party was determined to hold on to power because he had the support of the country's House of Representatives (the lower house of Parliament). Opposition leader Malcolm Fraser of the Liberal Party used his party's majority in the Senate (the upper house) to block bills that allowed tax money to be spent.

Whitlam called for a half-Senate election, believing that the result would allow bills to pass through the Senate again. On November 11, 1975, he announced his intention to the governor-general, Sir John Kerr. Usually, such an announcement would be a formality and immediately approved by the queen's representative. Instead, the governor-general dismissed Whitlam and replaced him with Fraser. A general election was called on December 13, and Fraser's Liberal Party won.

Sir John Kerr believed that his actions were the only way to solve the problem and to produce a strong decisive government. Many Australians, however, believed that he went well beyond his official role in dismissing an elected government. What do you think?

Changing Times

Centuries ago, monarchies were the most common form of government in Europe and beyond. Everyone, from the monarch to the poorest farm worker, knew his or her place. Today, the concept of monarchy is changing, which leads to many questions.

• What place do monarchies have in the twenty-first century?
• Are monarchies out of step with the modern world?
• Does a system of kings and queens, princes and princesses exist simply to attract tourists to palaces and royal events?
• Might reigning monarchs have more than a symbolic role?

Most monarchies have managed to find answers to these questions that suit the needs and attitudes of their nation. The British expect their royal family to be formal, adding a traditional presence to ceremonies at home and state trips to foreign countries. Especially since economic times have become harder, the British royal family has become more open about its wealth and earnings. It has had to learn from public relations mistakes such as the TV program *The Grand Knockout Tournament* in 1987 (see pages 40–41) and the funeral of Diana, Princess of Wales, 10 years later (see Voice of the People).

The British monarchy represents a formal approach. The monarchies of Scandinavia, the Netherlands, and Belgium are examples of comparatively informal monarchies. Those nations expect their royal families to be part of wider society, rather than seeming to stand above it. People sometimes use the term "bicycle monarchies" to describe those royal families. The phrase originated with Dutch Queen Juliana's habit of making unscheduled bike rides through the streets of Amsterdam.

Beyond Tradition and Pageantry

Today, monarchs have mainly symbolic roles in constitutional monarchies. It is easy to dismiss them as being simply decorative. At best, they play a politically neutral, unthreatening role as head of state.

Prince Charles, with his sons William and Harry, inspect the masses of flowers people left after the death of the young princes' mother, Diana, in August 1997.

THE PEOPLE'S PRINCESS

Diana, Princess of Wales, married Prince Charles in 1981, but the couple divorced in 1996. Diana was young and attractive and sometimes risked her life in her charity work. She seemed to breathe new life into the British monarchy. She remained popular after the divorce and the world was stunned when she died in a car accident in August 1997.

People displayed their grief openly and publicly in ways not usually associated with British reserve, yet the royal family seemed more removed from the public than usual in the days before her funeral. As the Independent *newspaper reported at the time, "If only the royals dared weep with the people."*

Tony Blair, prime minister at the time, was more in tune with public opinion, even finding a title for Diana that captured the mood: "People everywhere, not just here in Britain, kept faith with Princess Diana. They liked her, they loved her, they regarded her as one of the people. She was the People's Princess and that is how she will stay, how she will remain in our hearts and our memories for ever."

Even in the twenty-first century, some monarchs have played an important part in preserving political calm. Belgium's monarchy, like the country itself, is less than 200 years old. But the country faces serious divisions between its French-speaking (Walloon) population and its Flemish (Dutch) speakers. At times, tensions between these groups threaten to tear the country apart. King Albert II has arranged many meetings between the two groups to help rebuild unity.

In Thailand, pro-democracy protesters, known as red shirts, clashed with police and soldiers in early 2010. The army had responded violently to protests in Bangkok and other cities, and some observers predicted a civil war. But King Bumiphol had the respect of both sides and helped cool the tension enough to stop the violence and find political solutions.

A Thai Red Shirt protest rocks Bangkok in March 2010. Many observers credit the country's king with preventing an all-out civil war.

MELINE... TIMELINE... TIMELINE... TIMELINE... TIMELINE... TIMELINE...

| AD 1793 | Execution of King Louis XVI ends the French monarchy |

Heirs to the Throne

British Prime Minister David Cameron became leader of the Conservative Party in 2005, only four years after being elected to Parliament for the first time. Barack Obama, elected US president in 2008, had been a US senator since only 2004 and had served in the Illinois Senate for seven years before that. Many people believed —and still believe—that Cameron and Obama lack the experience to lead their countries.

Are public attitudes different toward those who are born into, rather than elected, to leadership roles? The notion of job training is one area where the monarchy scores highly. While many people disagree with minor royals being given handouts from taxpayers' money, fewer people criticize the money spent on those likely to inherit the throne.

In some ways, being a royal is like being born in a bygone era when sons and daughters knew from childhood they would spend their adult lives doing what their parents did. A prince could imagine being king in the same way that a coal miner's son could expect to work down the mines or a maid's daughter might follow in her mother's footsteps.

Prince Charles (left) with his sons Harry (center) and William (right) take part in a game of polo, a sport that is also known as "the sport of kings."

MEETING THE PEOPLE

Most Russians agree that Peter the Great (1672–1725) was their finest tsar. Standing nearly 6 feet 6 inches (2 m) tall, he towered over those around him and had a powerful personality. He built a modern new capital, Saint Petersburg, and reorganized many aspects of Russian society and government. As a young man, he traveled across Europe, staying in Germany, the Netherlands, and England as he learned about shipbuilding, navies, architecture, and many other subjects.

Since Peter's time, royal families have tried to find the best way to occupy heirs to the throne. Few have been as ambitious as Peter, who apparently traveled in secret. Most princes become associated with one of the armed forces. In Britain, Prince William and Prince Harry have been given high-profile military training. Their father, Prince Charles, trained in the air force and navy, but also became the first member of the British royal family to study for a university degree, which he was awarded by Cambridge University in 1970.

IMELINE... TIMELINE... TIMELINE... TIMELINE... TIMELINE... TIMELINE...

| 1814 | Norwegian and Swedish monarchies unite | 1848 | Dutch constitutional monarchy formed |

The new generation of royals are taking on real jobs—often very dangerous and in the public eye. Felipe de Bourbon, crown prince of Spain (heir to the Spanish throne), is a trained military helicopter pilot.

VOICE OF THE PEOPLE

SHARED EMOTIONS

It is easy to forget that privileged royals suffer some of the same joys and pain of other people. In 2009, Britain's Prince William became royal patron of the Child Bereavement Charity, which his mother (Diana, Princess of Wales) had supported. Her death in 1997 left William and his brother Harry devastated: "Never being able to say the word 'mummy' again in your life sounds like a small thing. However, for many, including me, it's now really just a word—hollow and evoking memories."

TIMELINE... TIMELINE... TIMELINE... TIMELINE... TIMELINE... TIMELIN

AD **1871**   German Empire established   **1905**   Norwegian and Swedish monarchies separate

On-the-job Training

A childhood growing up in a royal household might seem full of advantages with travel, wealth, and people ready to run all sorts of errands. But it is also very limiting. Imagine never being able to jump on a bike and ride to a friend's house or to decide on the spur of the moment to go to a restaurant or movie. The need for security means that all royals are watched over constantly.

As well as being watched, young members of a royal family begin to accompany their parents at public functions: opening museums and schools, watching awards ceremonies, visiting schools and hospitals, and so on. In a typical year, there might be as many as 400 functions. A prince or princess who began attending functions from the age of 12, will be very experienced when the time comes to inherit the throne.

The question of how—and when—to prepare for the role as a monarch is very tricky in the modern world (see The Voting Booth). Removing young royals from official duties to give them more life experience also runs the risk of leaving them unprepared when the time comes to assume royal duties.

THE VOTING BOOTH

Preparation

In addition to showing that they have had the right experience to govern, political leaders are often criticized for being out of touch with ordinary voters or the real world. Unlike politicians of 40 or 50 years ago (who might have run companies, worked in mines, or been soldiers before entering politics), modern politicians have usually spent their entire adulthood in politics.

Do you think that the same accusation of being out of touch is true of a country's royal family? Can you think of some way in which royals could share more of the experiences of their subjects? Or do they do enough already?

TIMELINE... TIMELINE... TIMELINE... TIMELINE... TIMELINE... TIMELINE...

| 1910 | Portuguese monarchy overthrown | 1912 | Pu Yi, China's last emperor **abdicates** |

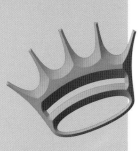

End of the Line

If people are unhappy with their prime minister or president, voters can remove them at the next election. Democratic government remains, but the new leader (or governing party) can still make sweeping changes. Replacing a king or queen is a different matter; it is more common to depose an entire monarchy than to replace a reigning monarch.

VOICE
OF THE
PEOPLE

EXECUTING THE ROMANOVS

The execution of the Russian royal family (the Romanovs) on July 17, 1918, followed a brutal logic. The new communist government, which had seized power during the revolution, knew that Tsar Nicholas II and his family were symbols of the monarchy. The country was in the middle of a civil war and pro-monarchy forces were trying to rescue the Romanovs. The communists wanted to make sure the monarchy could not be restored if they were defeated.

By mid-July 1918, the Romanovs had been moved to Ekaterinburg, which is 1,645 miles (2,650 km) away from Saint Petersburg and 1,200 miles (1,933 km) away from Moscow. As pro-monarchy forces closed in on Ekaterinburg, the government decided to execute the royal family and dispose of their bodies.

Pavel Medvedev was a member of the squad of soldiers who guarded the Romanovs. He later described how the royal family entered the room where they would soon be shot: "The maid carried a pillow. The tsar's daughters also brought small pillows with them. One pillow was put on the empress's chair; another on the heir's chair. It seemed as if all of them guessed their fate, but not one of them uttered a single sound. At this moment eleven men entered the room: Yurovsky [head of the execution squad], his assistant, two members of the Extraordinary Commission [local revolutionary government], and seven [secret police]."

An elderly Russian holds an icon (sacred image) of Nicholas II, Russia's last tsar. Many Russians believe that Nicholas, who was murdered during the Russian Revolution, is a saint.

Off with Their Heads

Political revolutions have overthrown many monarchies over the centuries, even though some countries later reversed their actions. However, representatives of England's Parliament executed King Charles I during the English civil war. Louis XVI and his wife Marie-Antoinette were victims of the French Revolution; and Tsar Nicholas II and his entire family were shot during the Russian Revolution.

In these cases, anti-monarchy forces realized how powerful a symbol a living king or queen (or tsar) could be. In less chaotic circumstances, once-powerful monarchs can live out their lives in comfort. In 1918, **Kaiser** Wilhelm II fled to the Netherlands when revolution was about to overthrow the German monarchy. Dutch Queen Wilhelmina

TIMELINE... TIMELINE... TIMELINE... TIMELINE... TIMELINE... TIMELINE...

| 1918 | Austro-Hungarian kingdom, German Empire abolished | 1931 | Spanish monarchy overthrown |

Norodom Sihanouk offers up a prayer at the Silver Pagoda in Phnom Penh, Cambodia's capital, shortly after his return from 13 years' exile in 1991.

refused to expel him (to face trial for **war crimes**). The former kaiser bought a mansion. Soon after Wilhelm's exile, however, the German government allowed him back into the country to collect his things. He returned to the Netherlands with more than two dozen railway cars full of belongings—including a car and a boat. He died in 1941.

TIMELINE... TIMELINE... TIMELINE... TIMELINE... TIMELINE... TIMELINE

AD 1952   British Queen Elizabeth II takes the thron   1970   Cambodian monarchy overthrown

RETURN OF THE KING

The German political philosopher Karl Marx (1818–83) and his followers (Marxists) believed that human history was predictable. Marx argued that change took place because of a constant struggle between social **classes** to gain power. According to his view, the idea of monarchy had become outdated by the time **feudalism** had developed in the ninth century in the Middle Ages. Capitalism (the system that encourages individuals to set up their own businesses) replaced feudalism in the Middle Ages as the rising merchant class wanted the freedom to go into business.

In Marx's view, capitalism would eventually fall apart as the working class (which produced the goods) gained power. Marx predicted that communism would replace capitalism by the twentieth century. Imagine the surprise of Marxist political experts when countries returned to monarchies despite having gotten rid of their kings and queens earlier.

Britain restored its monarchy in 1660 after a civil war and 11 years of parliamentary rule. The new king, Charles II, was aware that the role of monarch had returned by popular request and that he needed to respect British public opinion. Approximately 25 years later, the British welcomed another king (William III) from the Netherlands. However, the strict controls over the monarchy that Parliament put in place in 1688 drastically reduced the king's political power.

In the late twentieth century, two other countries that had suffered civil wars turned back to their monarchies as a way of healing national wounds. Spain's civil war in the 1930s led to more than three decades of military dictatorship under General Franco. In 1975, when Franco died, the country welcomed King Juan Carlos to the monarchy. Cambodia had a turbulent period during the 1970s when the Khmer Rouge (an extremist communist government) murdered millions of civilians. In 1993, Norodom Sihanouk was returned to the Cambodian throne to preside over a constitutional monarchy when the Khmer Rouge leaders were driven from the country.

IMELINE... TIMELINE... TIMELINE... TIMELINE... TIMELINE... TIMELINE...

1975   Spanish monarchy restored   1993   Cambodian monarchy restored

Monarchy and the Media

British TV viewers saw an unusual royal spectacle on June 15, 1987. Several of the queen's children, plus an assortment of celebrities, were involved in a comic game show called *The Grand Knockout Tournament*. Prince Edward, Princess Anne, and the Duke and Duchess of York (Prince Andrew and his wife, Sarah Ferguson) were captains of celebrity teams, which competed in a series of silly contests. The wacky games were based on those in a popular television game show called *It's a Knockout.*

Huge crowds, photographers, and reporters from around the world gather outside Buckingham Palace on July 29, 1981, on the occasion of Prince Charles's wedding to Lady Diana Spencer.

PUBLIC RELATIONS

Image—how the public views a person or organization—is an important feature of modern politics. Skilled politicians can make sure that voters learn about any news story that makes them look good: consoling victims of disasters, being present when a national sportsperson wins a world championship, and so on. They use a technique called **spin** to play down stories that are less favorable to them.

These are examples of public relations (PR), which monarchies depend on as much as elected governments do. Their success is often measured in terms of how the public reacts. Prince Edward's celebrity television program was poor PR, as were the royal divorces of Prince Charles, Prince Andrew, and Princess Anne.

More recently, Britain's royal family has improved its PR in an area that is important to many taxpayers—money. Since 1993, the queen has paid income tax as everyone else in Britain. Other royals have published much clearer accounts of how they spend their money.

One game had team members dressed as giant vegetables, throwing plastic hams at each other. Another had players dressed as **jesters** shimmying across a slippery log above a pool of water. The event succeeded in raising more than $1.652 million (£1 million) for favorite royal charities, but most people remember it as an embarrassing failure. The original program, with ordinary people falling about, shouting, and being splashed seemed like harmless nonsense. The royal version, with people laughing a little too loudly at jokes that were never very funny, came across as forced and undignified.

Afterward, Prince Edward (who had suggested the idea) asked reporters what they thought of the event. When no reply came, Prince Edward stormed out of the room, thanking them sarcastically for their appreciation.

The Power of Television

For many observers of the British monarchy, Prince Edward's television special marked a turning point. Before that, people in Britain and beyond had been fascinated by and respected the British monarchy. Members of the royal family sometimes appeared on television, but they were usually opening public buildings or offering support to charities. People were especially fascinated by the pageantry of the monarchy such as Queen Elizabeth's coronation in 1953, her Silver Jubilee in 1977, and the wedding of Prince Charles and Lady Diana Spencer in 1981.

Almost overnight, Edward seemed to have lowered the monarchy from its previous respected position to the level of pop singers and soap stars. No one was happy with the result. Monarchists believed that the change removed the dignity of the monarchy. Others believed that the royal family was simply unfunny and the program failed to give it the popularity that Edward had hoped for.

British people sometimes refer to their royal family as "The Firm" because of its huge size and influence. The comparison is surprisingly accurate. Like any major company, it has a management structure and someone sitting firmly at the top of it all (the reigning monarch). Like modern companies, the royal family has become aware of the image it presents to the outside world. Many people believe that the wedding of Prince William to Catherine Middleton in 2011 helped restore some of the royal family's timeless attraction without making it seem too stuffy and old-fashioned.

TWENTY-FIRST CENTURY BATTLE LINES

People have argued for and against monarchies for centuries. It shouldn't be surprising that many of the fiercest arguments are now conducted on the Internet through blogs, on official websites (both pro- and anti-monarchy), and through social networking sites such as Twitter. In November 2010, the British monarchy created a Facebook fan page to post news and events of the royal family.

The Royals and the Media

Many people believe that reporters and celebrity photographers (known as paparazzi) go too far in their coverage of Britain's royal family. They argue that the royals have less privacy than ordinary individuals. Some believe that the persistence of these photographers led to the car crash in which Princess Diana died in 1997.

Others believe that if taxpayers fund the royal family's travel, palaces, and extravagant lifestyle, they should be informed about how their money is spent—especially during troubled economic times when so many ordinary people are struggling. Do you think that the media interferes with the royals too much?

The wreckage of the car in which Princess Diana died is pulled from the tunnel in Paris where it crashed at high speed.

Looking Ahead

In the 2,500 years since the Romans replaced their monarchy with a republic, people have predicted the end of monarchies. Yet they still survive in the twenty-first century. Few monarchs wield real power, but monarchies provide many people with a comforting sense of tradition and order, which might be the key to their survival.

MEASURING MONARCHIES

Is the idea of maintaining a monarchy—with the palaces and pageantry—a waste of money in difficult economic times? Monarchists refer to the Legatum Institute, an international organization that "researches and promotes the principles that drive the creation of global prosperity and the expansion of human liberty." Every year, it examines the factors that allow countries to become prosperous with happy inhabitants. The factors include health, safety and security, education, and personal freedom. The top 15 countries in the 2011 list (based on a combination of all the factors listed above) are:

1. *Norway*
2. *Denmark*
3. *Australia*
4. *New Zealand*
5. Sweden
6. *Canada*
7. Finland
8. Switzerland
9. *Netherlands*
10. United States
11. Ireland
12. Iceland
13. *United Kingdom*
14. Austria
15. Germany

More than half these countries— those in *italics*—are monarchies. Seven of the top ten and four of the top five countries are monarchies. Of the 15 countries in this list, Queen Elizabeth is the monarch of the United Kingdom, Australia, Canada, and New Zealand.

VOICE OF THE PEOPLE

CITIZENS' VIEWS

This contribution to a website called the Commonwealth conversation is from Massachusetts and a supporter of monarchy: "I look at my cocitizens today in the world's banner republic, and I see no traditions. I see a vast horde easily swayed by fear. I see not men but livestock. Republics degenerate into mob rule. Seriously, look at our presidents; I'd not fight or die for any of them over the past 20 years! But for a monarch, a not partisan figure who represents all that is good and honourable about one's country, I'd gladly go to war!"

On the other hand, one of Britain's best-loved cookery writers, Delia Smith, wrote in the Times *in 2009: "I'm not anti the queen. But monarchy in general, I can't see the point. Because I believe everybody is equal, I can't believe in having to walk backwards . . . . What I do believe in is leadership."*

Lord Irvine, a senior cabinet member, bows to Queen Elizabeth at an official function in 2000. Will such a gesture seem outdated in 25 years time?

Glossary

abdicate   To formally give up royal duties.

absolute monarch   A monarch who has complete political power over a country.

Austro-Hungarian Empire   An empire that combined the monarchies of Austria and Hungary from 1867 to 1918.

bill   The wording of a new law presented to a law-making body such as Parliament for approval.

carbuncle   A large, painful, and unattractive swelling under the skin.

citizen   A member of a society in which everyone has the same rights and duties and no one has special privileges.

Civil List   The annual amount of money that Parliament gives to the British royal family and royal household.

class   A group of people, such as merchants or nobles, sharing a social or economic position.

College of Cardinals   The group of cardinals (most senior clergy) of the Catholic Church that elects a new pope after the death of the previous pope.

Commonwealth of Nations   An international organization of 54 independent countries (most of which were once ruled by Britain) that work together to promote peaceful development.

communism   A political system in which all property is owned by the community and each person contributes and receives according to their ability and needs. A communist government provides work, health care, education, and housing, but may deny people certain freedoms.

compromise   The settlement of a dispute in which each side gives ground to the other.

Congress   The elected law-making body of the United States, consisting of the House of Representatives and the Senate.

constitutional monarchy   A form of government in which the monarch acts as head of state, but elected officials have political power.

democracy   A form of government in which people choose political leaders by voting.

dynasty   A series of rulers from the same family.

emir   An independent ruler of a Muslim country.

feudalism   A system of government in which nobles gave people land and protection; in return, they worked and fought for the noble.

free press   The legal right of newspapers, television, radio, and other communicators to report events without government control.

governor-general   An appointed representative of the British monarch in a country that recognizes the monarch as its head of state.

head of state   The person who represents the state (or nation) in public affairs.

heredity (in monarchies)   Passing power from parent to child or to another relative when a monarch dies.

Holy Roman Emperor   The ruler of a group of lands in Central and Western Europe (mainly in what is now Germany); the Holy Roman Empire lasted from AD 843 to 1806.

jester   A monarch's personal clown.

kaiser   The ruler of the German Empire, which lasted from 1871 to 1918.

majority   Having more than half the seats in a law-making body such as Parliament.

Napoleon   Napoleon Bonaparte (1769–1821) was a military leader who ruled France from 1799 to 1812 and conquered much of Europe.

noble   A member of the nobility, the social class just below the monarch.

parricidal   Related to the killing of one or both parents.

pharaoh   The monarch in ancient Egypt.

Queen's Speech   A speech, written by the elected government and outlining political plans, read by the British monarch at the opening of each session of Parliament.

referendum   A proposed change to the law put to voters to decide before it can take effect.

republic   A form of democracy in which voters exercise power through their elected representatives and head of state.

revolution   A sudden political change in which an existing government is overthrown by the people who are governed.

royal household   The staff who work with and for monarchs and their immediate family members.

between 1939 and 1945.

spin   Presentation of news stories to play up successes and play down setbacks.

standard   The flag or other symbol of a nation.

sultan   The monarch of a Muslim country.

tsar   The title of the Russian monarch.

war crime   An act of cruelty that goes beyond internationally accepted codes of warfare.

World War I   The war fought mainly in Europe between 1914 and 1918.

World War II   The war that began in Europe and spread around the world between 1939 and 1945.

Books

Tames, Richard. *Monarchy (Political and Economic Systems).* Heinemann, 2008.

Harris, Nathaniel. *Monarchy (Systems of Government).* World Almanac Library, 2005.

Cox, Alexander, Deborah Lock, Fleur Star (eds). *Who's In Charge?* Dorling Kindersley, 2010.

Websites

Australian Republic
http://www.republic.org.au

British Monarchy – official website
http://www.royal.gov.uk/Home.aspx

Australians for Constitutional Monarchy
http://www.norepublic.com.au

The Commonwealth Secretariat
http://www.thecommonwealth.org

Index